UNDER OHIO

UNDER OHIO

THE STORY OF OHIO'S ROCKS AND FOSSILS

Written and illustrated by

Charles Ferguson Barker

OHIO UNIVERSITY PRESS

ATHENS

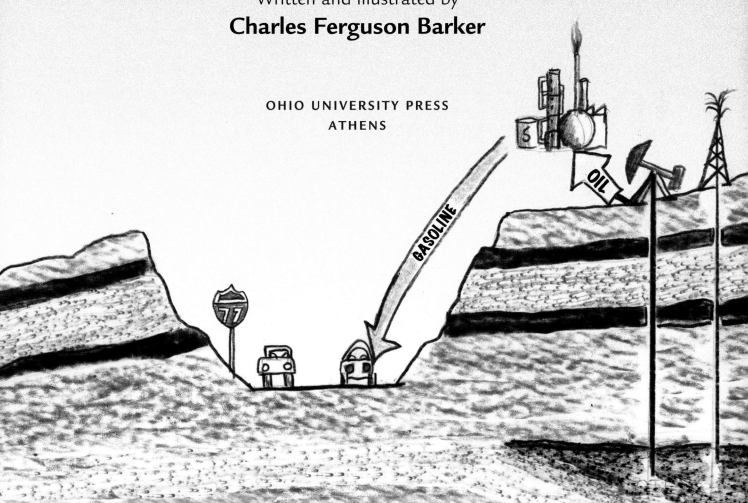

Ohio University Press, Athens, Ohio 45701
www.ohio.edu/oupress
© 2007 by Charles Ferguson Barker

Printed in China

14 13 12 11 10 09 08 07   5 4 3 2 1

Under Ohio: The Story of Ohio's Rocks and Fossils is an adaptation of *Under Michigan: The Story of Michigan's Rocks and Fossils* by Charles Ferguson Barker and is published by arrangement with Wayne State University Press.

ACKNOWLEDGMENTS

There are many people to thank for making this book possible. Thanks go to David Sanders and all the people at Ohio University Press as well as to the anonymous reviewers of the draft manuscript for their helpful input. Don Guy, geologist with the Ohio Department of Natural Resources (ODNR) Division of Geological Survey, pointed me to the many informative publications on Ohio geology by the ODNR. Madge Fitak kindly sent me many of those publications. Many thanks are owed to Gregory A. Schumacher, geologist with the ODNR Division of Geological Survey, who, with little advance notice, provided many useful comments and suggestions for the manuscript with a lightning-fast response. Events that occurred hundreds of millions of years ago may always be up for debate, and I accept full responsibility for my presentation of them here. Finally, thanks go to my wife Peg and to little Clare for giving me encouragement to uncover and explore the fascinating geology of Ohio.

Library of Congress Cataloging-in-Publication Data

Barker, Charles Ferguson.
 Under Ohio : the story of Ohio's rocks and fossils / Charles Ferguson Barker. —1st.
   p. cm.
 ISBN-13: 978-0-8214-1755-3 (cloth : alk. paper)
 ISBN-10: 0-8214-1755-X (cloth : alk. paper)
 1. Geology—Ohio—Juvenile literature. 2. Geology, Stratigraphic—Juvenile literature.
 3. Fossils—Ohio—Juvenile literature.
 I. Title.

QE151.B37 2007
557.71—dc22

                                                    2007006876

For Clare

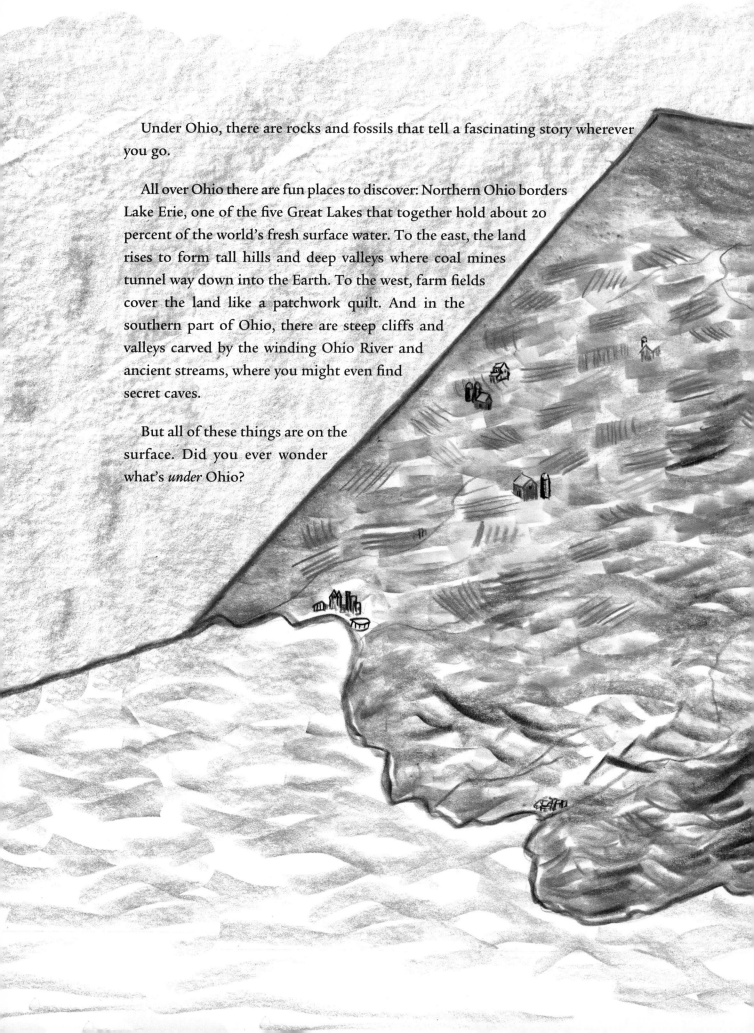

Under Ohio, there are rocks and fossils that tell a fascinating story wherever you go.

All over Ohio there are fun places to discover: Northern Ohio borders Lake Erie, one of the five Great Lakes that together hold about 20 percent of the world's fresh surface water. To the east, the land rises to form tall hills and deep valleys where coal mines tunnel way down into the Earth. To the west, farm fields cover the land like a patchwork quilt. And in the southern part of Ohio, there are steep cliffs and valleys carved by the winding Ohio River and ancient streams, where you might even find secret caves.

But all of these things are on the surface. Did you ever wonder what's *under* Ohio?

You might be surprised by all the different kinds of rocks and fossils under Ohio.

There are rocks from magma that cooled slowly underground.

There are rocks from fiery volcanoes that erupted over the land when continents pulled apart.

There are rocks from mountains that towered over Ohio when continents pushed together.

There are rocks from tropical seas that covered Ohio millions of years ago and left behind fossil seashells, corals, and fish bones.

And there are rocks left behind by icy-cold glaciers that spread across the land—you might even find diamonds or gold among the glacier-scraped stones.

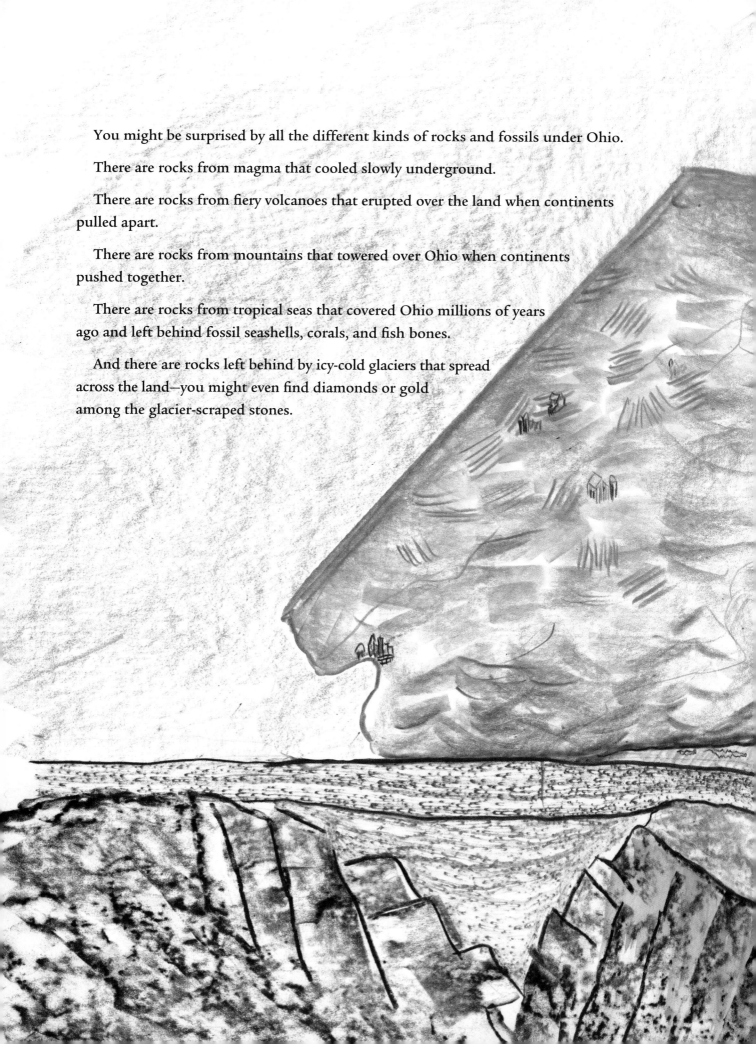

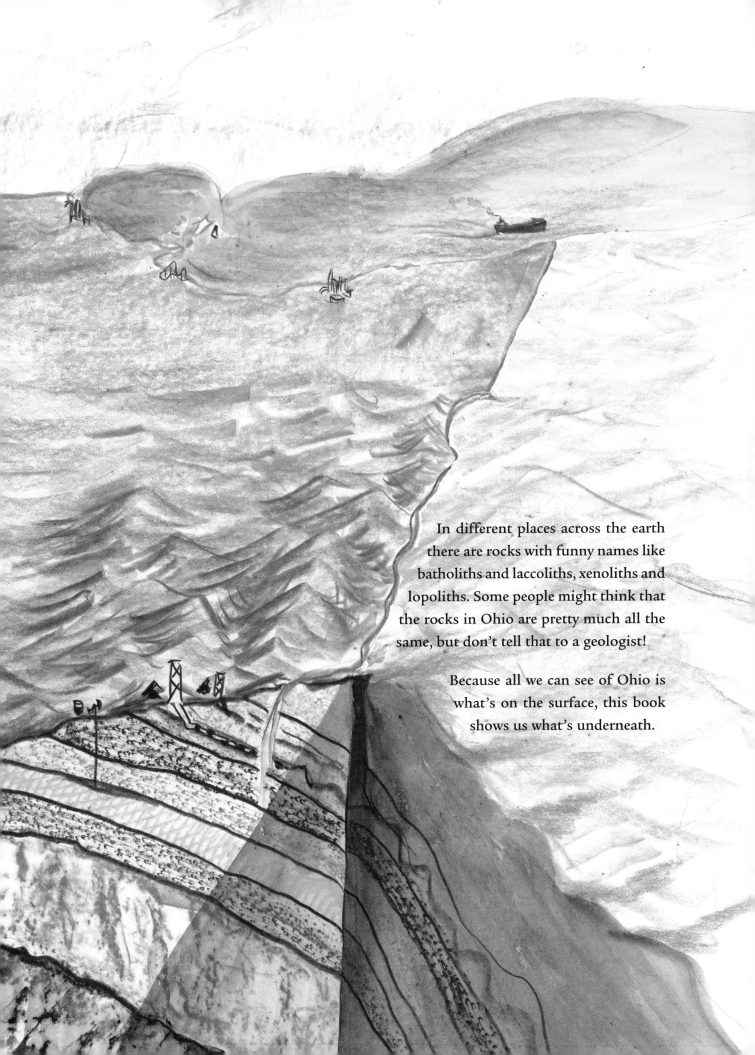

In different places across the earth there are rocks with funny names like batholiths and laccoliths, xenoliths and lopoliths. Some people might think that the rocks in Ohio are pretty much all the same, but don't tell that to a geologist!

Because all we can see of Ohio is what's on the surface, this book shows us what's underneath.

OHIO'S BEGINNINGS

The story of the rocks and fossils under Ohio goes back almost four and a half billion years to when the Earth was born. Back before there were any human beings or even any plants or animals—back when there were only rocks and seas and air. The oldest rocks in Ohio are under the western part of the state and are more than a billion years old. But they are buried thousands of feet deep under thick layers of younger rocks.

To tell the story of the rocks and fossils in Ohio and around the world, geologists divide time from the beginning of the Earth right up to now into different periods—just as we have names for months of the year and days of the week.

Geologic time is so long that the periods are divided by major events in Earth history, like when certain plants or animals showed up or when others became extinct.

The rocks and fossils under Ohio are from many different time periods. Some formed billions of years ago, and some are just starting to form now under lakes and streams—and maybe in your own backyard. But rocks from some time periods, like those from the age of the dinosaurs, are simply missing. That may be either because water and wind swept the rocks and fossils away or because the land was slowly rising during that time and no thick layers of rocks and fossils were deposited. Without rocks or fossils as clues to the past, we can only guess what happened!

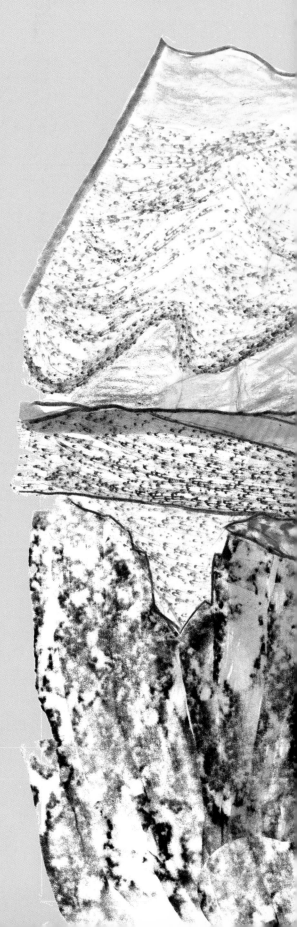

NAME OF TIME PERIOD	YEARS AGO	WHAT WAS HAPPENING THEN

Your birthday

Glaciers cover northern and western Ohio

QUATERNARY

1,800,000

TERTIARY

65,000,000 — Dinosaurs extinct

CRETACEOUS

145,000,000 — No rocks in Ohio from this time

JURASSIC

213,000,000

TRIASSIC

248,000,000 — Trilobites extinct

PERMIAN

Western Ohio pushed up

286,000,000

PENNSYLVANIAN

325,000,000 — Swamps that later turn to coal

MISSISSIPPIAN

360,000,000

DEVONIAN — Seas cover Ohio

410,000,000

SILURIAN

440,000,000

ORDOVICIAN

505,000,000 — First fish

CAMBRIAN

544,000,000

Grenville Mountains over Ohio

PRECAMBRIAN

Ohio splits apart, then stops

4,500,000,000 — Earth is born

Under Ohio, you can find all three of the main types of rock in the world: igneous, sedimentary, and metamorphic.

Igneous rocks are found deep under Ohio (the deepest rocks are actually called "basement rocks"). Igneous rocks are formed when magma or lava cools and crystallizes. They can cool slowly under the surface as plutonic rock, or they can shoot up onto the land and cool quickly as volcanic rock.

We can't see the deep igneous rocks of Ohio because they are covered by other layers of rocks left by ancient seas. We know they are there from samples taken from wells drilled deep under Ohio. But we can also find pieces of igneous rocks, such as small cobbles or pebbles, at the surface in some places. Glaciers picked up these rocks in Canada as they moved southward and dropped them on Ohio when the thick ice melted.

Sedimentary rocks form when other rocks break up into small bits of sand, silt, and clay called "sediment." The sediments are moved by streams, glaciers, or winds and finally settle down in oceans or lakes, or on the land. The sediments pile up on top of each other like clothes on the floor of a messy room. Over time, the small grains of sand, silt, and clay can become compressed and cemented together. This turns the loose bits of sediment (like sand on a beach) into sedimentary rocks that can be as hard as a sidewalk. Ohio has lots of places to see layers of sedimentary rock where roads or rivers cut through the hills.

IGNEOUS ROCKS
(including volcanic rocks)

Sedimentary rocks can also form when a sea dries up and leaves layers of salt and other types of rock (a mine under Cleveland goes down more than a thousand feet to a buried layer of salt). Ohio's sedimentary rocks include coal, limestone, sandstone, and shale. They also include flint—Ohio's official gemstone—which was used to make arrowheads and jewelry for thousands of years!

Sometimes pieces of plants or the shells, bones, or teeth of animals settle down with the sediment and eventually become part of the rock, where they can turn into fossils. Or sometimes an animal might leave only tracks when it walked across muddy land or crawled on the sea bottom.

Ohio also has **metamorphic rocks** that are found mostly deep underground. Metamorphic rocks are made from other existing rocks that have been changed by heat and pressure when buried deep or when hot molten rock moves in next to them (metamorphic simply means "changed"—like a caterpillar that metamorphoses into a butterfly).

We can't see lots of metamorphic rocks at the surface of Ohio because they are buried deep, but we can find small pieces of metamorphic rocks that were brought down from Canada by the glaciers, just like the pieces of igneous rocks.

SEDIMENTARY ROCKS

METAMORPHIC ROCKS

OHIO ON THE MOVE

Some of the layers of rocks and fossils under Ohio were formed in tropical seas like the ones that exist today near the equator. But how could Ohio have warm tropical seas covering it all year long when it gets so cold and snowy in the winter? It's because Ohio wasn't always where it is today. A long, long time ago, Ohio was farther south, where the weather is hot all year long. Although we can't feel it, the continents (and Ohio) have been moving over the Earth through time. That explains why, millions of years ago, Ohio was near and even *south* of the equator!

Continents move because the crust of the Earth is made up of huge plates of rock, like the parts of a cracked eggshell. The plates drift around the Earth with the continents riding on their backs. The plates move very slowly, though—about as slow as your fingernails grow! If you look at a globe, you can see that the coastlines of South America and Africa look like they could fit together like pieces of a jigsaw puzzle. That's because they *did* fit together once. The huge plates of the Earth slowly smash together, then pull apart or slide past each other over millions of years—all of this happened under Ohio too!

Someday, after millions and millions of years, all the continents will probably come back together again, and Ohio might be back near the equator and covered by a warm tropical sea once more. But not before many more cold Ohio winters have come and gone!

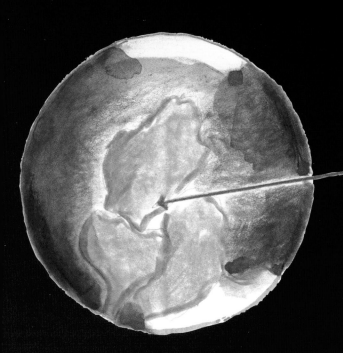

300 MILLION YEARS AGO

Ohio was here, south of the equator. It was hot! Swamps grew that later formed coal.

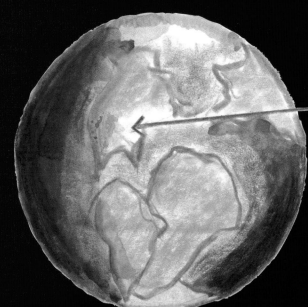

150 MILLION YEARS AGO

Ohio was here during the age of the dinosaurs.

TODAY

Ohio is here. (But we are slowly moving west!)

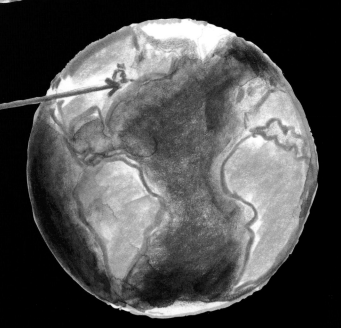

About a billion and a half years ago, the land under Ohio pushed up and then stretched out to the east and west as the North American continent began to split apart. The land stopped spreading apart about a billion years ago. If it hadn't, today we might have an ocean between eastern and western Ohio!

Some time after the land stopped pulling apart, another amazing thing happened: A continent smashed into Ohio and pushed up a huge mountain range called the Grenville Mountains. Those mountains were very tall and wide, and they stretched for thousands of miles. Wind and rain and streams and ice have long since worn those old mountains down, but we can still find their ancient roots deep under Ohio.

All this pulling and pushing of the land long ago caused cracks deep in the Earth's crust, and we still feel small earthquakes once in a while in Ohio. But there are not nearly as many earthquakes in Ohio as there are in California, where the big plates are still moving past each other!

OHIO'S FOSSILS

After all the ancient mountains were worn down flat more than 570 million years ago, shallow seas flowed across the land, covering Ohio and depositing layer upon layer of sedimentary rocks. Because Ohio was covered with tropical seas and beaches and swamps long, long ago, today we can find fossils of many types of creatures and plants that lived here in ancient times.

We can tell how old some of the layers of rock are by the types of fossils we find in them. That's because over long periods of time various types of plants and animals appear, become extinct, or change shape; so when they become fossilized, we can get an idea of when the rock formed. Ohio's state fossil is an extinct creature called a **trilobite.** It looked like a bug and used to live on the floor of tropical seas that covered Ohio starting around 570 million years ago.

We can find shells of clam-like animals called **brachiopods** that lived in the warm waters that covered Ohio millions of years ago.

We can find fossils of funny animals called **crinoids** that looked like flowers at the bottom of the seas—with stems like stacks of little buttons and tops like feathery petals.

And we can find fossil **corals** that lived in the bottom of those ancient oceans—some look like horns and are called "horn coral."

Limestone is a rock that often forms from the piling up of many fossils on the bottom of an ancient sea. Limestone is usually light gray in color and is sometimes used as a building stone, or crushed up to make concrete. So if you see a building made of big blocks of rock, look really close—you just might find some fossils!

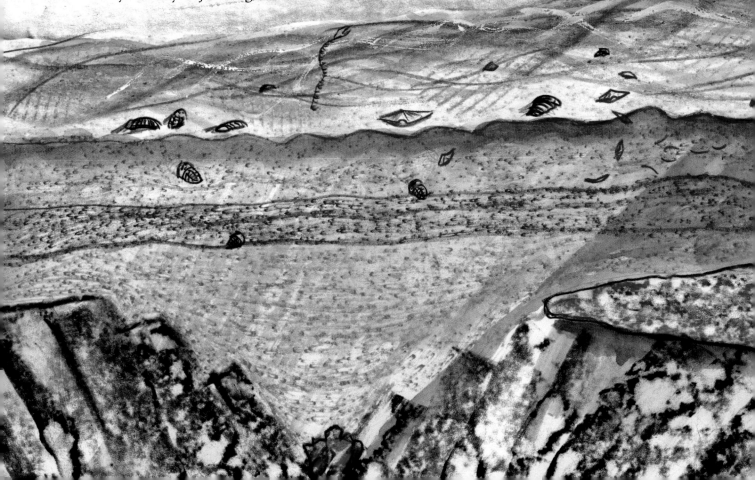

Ohio TimePike

Cretaceous Cleveland – 65 Million Years
Triassic Toledo – 213 Million Years
Devonian Dayton – 360 Million Years
Cambrian Cincinnati – 505 Million Years

About 300 million years ago, parts of the ancient Appalachian Mountains rose to the east of Ohio. As they wore down, rivers carried lots of sediment into the shallow sea that still covered much of Ohio. At the mouths of these rivers, sediment built huge deltas out into the sea, like the ones around New Orleans and the Mississippi River today. Back then it was hot all year long, and huge, steamy (and sometimes stinky) swamps covered much of eastern Ohio. As the plants in those old swamps fell into the water and were covered with more sediment, over a long time they were squashed down and became coal. If you look at the coal seams of eastern Ohio, sometimes you can see fossil plants from those old swamps.

Some microscopic organisms that lived in the ancient oceans were also buried, and after many years they turned into oil and natural gas. We use oil to make gasoline, heating oil, and even plastic!

NOW

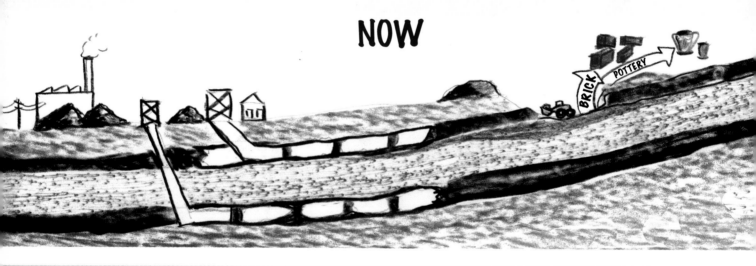

THEN
(300 million years ago)

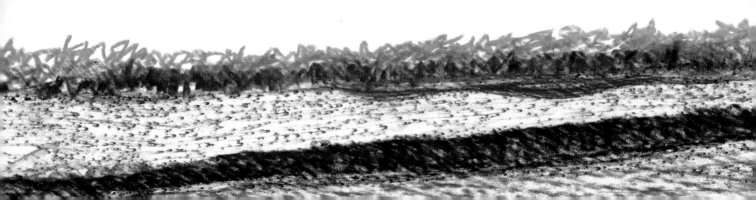

The very smallest pieces of sediment that settled in the quiet, still waters became layers of mud and clay. Some clay turned into a sedimentary rock called **shale,** which often contains the fossil remains of fish and other sea creatures. Some of Ohio's famous pottery and brick is made from this 300-million-year-old clay and shale. Companies in Cincinnati, Roseville, Zanesville, and many other Ohio towns have made beautiful pottery and bricks. Most bricks are red in color because the iron and other minerals in the clay turn red when they are heated up.

THEN
(300 million years ago)

Around 300 million years ago, the flat layers of sedimentary rock that had formed under the warm tropical seas were pushed up from below on the west side of Ohio.

The layers of rock were thrust upward, just as if you pushed your fist up below the edge of a stack of different-colored layers of Play-Doh—the oldest layers of Play-Doh (the ones at the bottom) can now be seen at the surface! This is why we see older rocks and fossils at or near the surface in the western part of the state and younger rocks as we go east.

OLDER ROCKS UNDER OHIO

YOUNGEST LAYER

OLDEST LAYER

YOUNGEST LAYER

OLDEST LAYER

YOUNGER ROCKS UNDER OHIO

YOUNGER LAYER

OLDER LAYER

OHIO UNDER ICE

Starting about 2 million years ago, the Earth's temperature cooled, and it snowed and snowed and snowed. It got so cold that the snow that fell during the long winters didn't melt completely during the cool summers.

Up in Canada, huge glaciers formed from all the snow that piled up and turned into ice. Soon the glaciers began to move southward. The glaciers were about a mile thick and soon covered most of northern and western Ohio, and some went even beyond Cincinnati!

The glaciers gouged out huge grooves in the rocks, like those we can see on Kelleys Island. In other places, we can see the sand, gravel, and clay left by the glaciers as they melted. These deposits blanket much of Ohio except for the high hills and valleys in the eastern part of the state. The glaciers even plucked up bits of diamond and gold as they scraped their way across Canada and dropped them far to the south. Sometimes glacial lakes, much bigger than Lake Erie is now, covered large parts of northern Ohio and created flat stretches of slippery clay. The last glacier melted completely about 10,000 years ago but left behind rolling hills and fine soils for farming in Ohio.

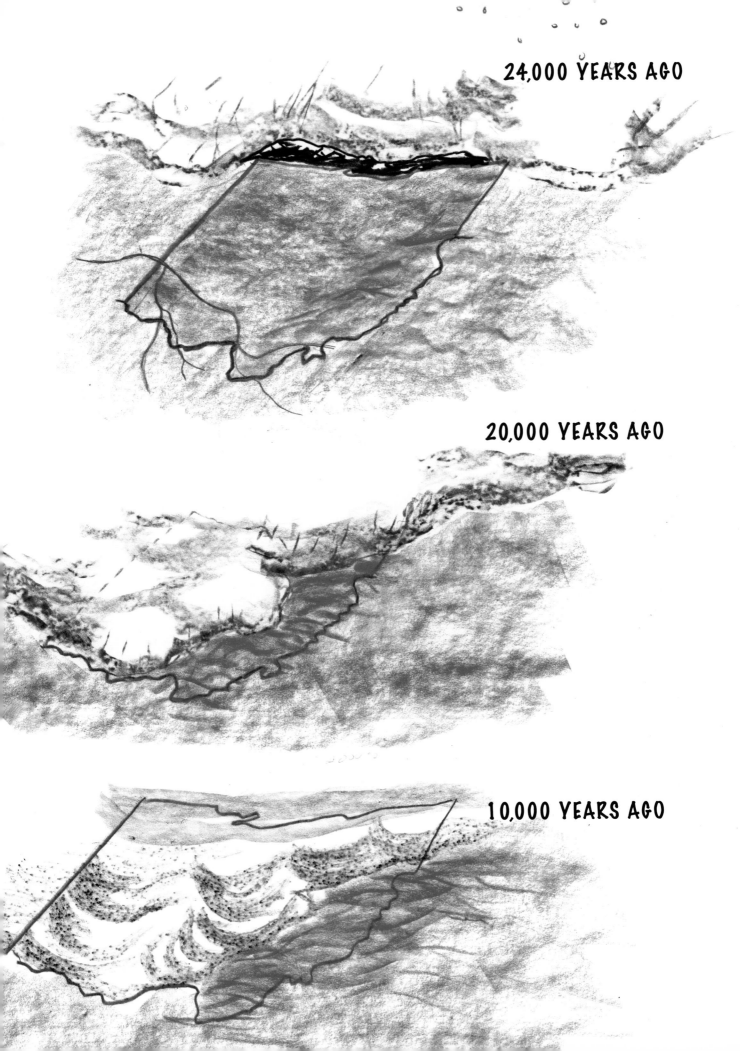

24,000 YEARS AGO

20,000 YEARS AGO

10,000 YEARS AGO

DISCOVER WHAT'S UNDER OHIO

So, from continents pulling apart and tall ancient mountains now worn down flat to warm tropical seas that covered the land and icy-cold glaciers that left behind boulders, clay, and sand, Ohio keeps changing again and again. That's why we have so many different rocks and fossils under Ohio—and that's why, wherever you go, there are all kinds of treasures to discover.

On Kelleys Island in Lake Erie, you can see huge, long grooves carved into the limestone bedrock by glaciers that moved down from Canada. These are some of the biggest and best glacial grooves found anywhere in the world!

Under Toledo is limestone from an ancient tropical sea. Relatives of Ohio's state fossil, the trilobite, are found in great numbers in the rocks exposed in large stone quarries just west of the city.

Under Campbell Hill, the highest point in Ohio (1,549 feet), the 400-million-year-old shale forms a hill that was so high and wide that it forced the big glaciers to move around it on each side.

Under Columbus, at the center of Ohio, deep under the sedimentary rocks that dip to the east, are the roots of the Grenville Mountains that were once higher than the Rockies!

Just north of Cincinnati, the last glacier stopped and left hills of sand and gravel. Under the city itself are some of the world's richest fossil beds, laid down by shallow seas that covered Ohio more than 400 million years ago. We can see rocks from those ancient seas in the cliffs cut by the Ohio River.

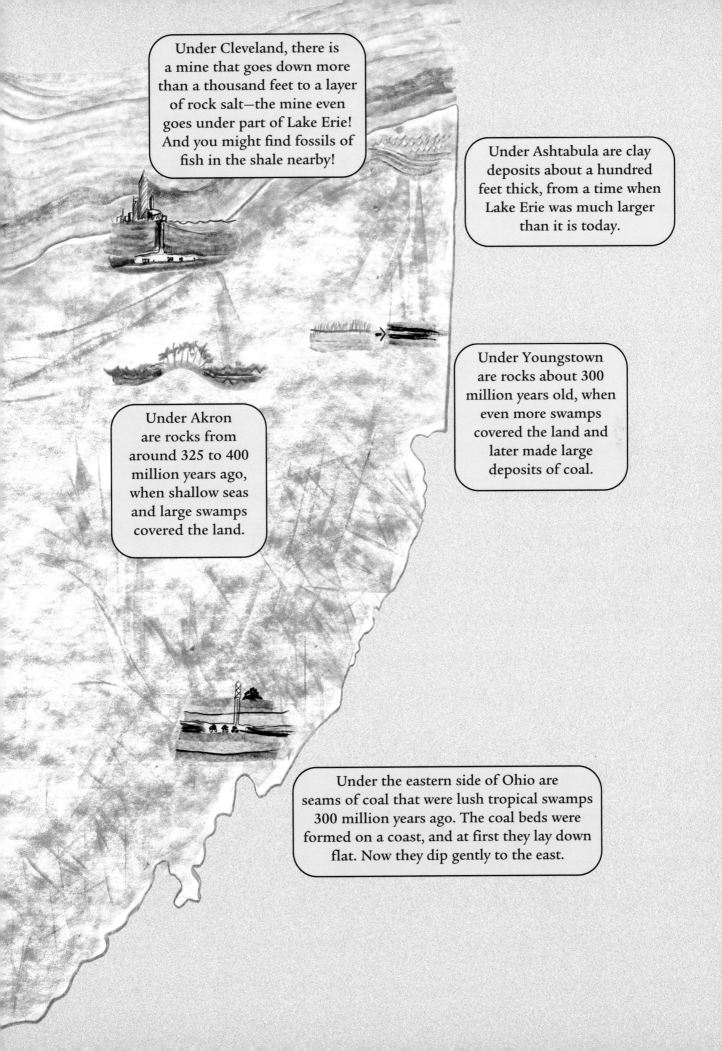

Under Ohio, there are all kinds of rocks and fossils. There are rocks and fossils from ancient tropical seas, and rocks from ancient mountains now long gone. There are rocks from volcanoes when the land split apart and rocks from magma that cooled slowly deep below. There are rocks from huge glaciers that bulldozed down from Canada.

But the story of the rocks and fossils of Ohio never ends. We don't know exactly when, but Ohio will be covered with volcanoes, tall mountains, warm tropical seas, and icy-cold glaciers once again!

If you look around Ohio, maybe even in your own backyard, you will find many interesting rocks and fossils from all kinds of times and places—and maybe, just maybe, you'll find some diamonds or gold. But best of all . . .

. . . you'll have fun just looking.

SOME COMMON ROCKS IN OHIO

SANDSTONE

Formed by beaches,
sand dunes,
river sediment

SHALE

Formed in
calm water

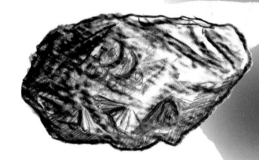

LIMESTONE

Formed in shallow
tropical seas—
look for fossils

GRANITE

Formed from slow-
cooling molten rock—
found deep under Ohio

BASALT

Formed from fast-
cooling volcanic rock

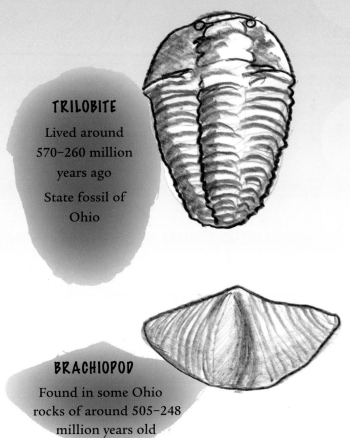

TRILOBITE

Lived around
570–260 million
years ago

State fossil of
Ohio

BRACHIOPOD

Found in some Ohio
rocks of around 505–248
million years old

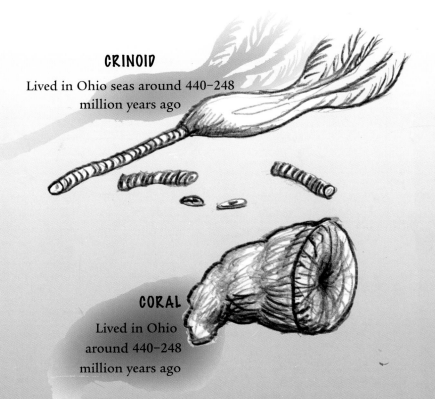

CRINOID

Lived in Ohio seas around 440–248
million years ago

CORAL

Lived in Ohio
around 440–248
million years ago

Glossary of Terms

batholith. Large mass of igneous rock that cools slowly below the Earth's surface.

brachiopod. Animal that lived in ancient oceans—fossils look like tiny clamshells that are stretched out at the sides.

coal. A sedimentary rock made up of very old plants that lived in swamps, were buried by sediment, and eventually compressed into a solid form. Sometimes called a "fossil fuel," along with oil and natural gas.

continent. Large landmass that rises above ocean basins—for example, North America.

coral. Mound of often colorful and sharp growths on the ocean floor made by marine organisms that live in shallow, warm seas.

crinoid. Animal that looked like a flower growing on the floor of ancient oceans.

crystallize. To turn into a solid form—like minerals that form as molten rock cools off.

Devonian. Geologic time period from about 408 to 360 million years ago.

dinosaurs. Extinct reptile that lived in the Mesozoic age of geologic time.

extinct. When something is gone for good.

flint. Sedimentary rock made mostly of quartz; Ohio's state gemstone.

fossil. Evidence of former life (parts of an animal, or its tracks) that eventually turned into rock. For example, an ancient shark's tooth, a seashell, or dinosaur footprints that are millions of years old.

glacier. Huge mass of ice that forms in cold climates where winter snow does not all melt in the summer.

Holocene. The name of the geologic time interval we are in now (started about 10,000 years ago).

igneous. Rocks that crystallize from magma (below the surface) or volcanic lava (above the surface).

Jurassic. Geologic time period from about 208 to 144 million years ago.

laccolith. A body of igneous rock that is shaped like an upside-down dish.

lava. Magma that erupts onto the Earth's surface.

limestone. A sedimentary rock usually formed in ocean environments.

lobe. Smaller part or "arm" of a larger glacier.

lopolith. Body of igneous rock shaped like a right-side-up dish.

magma. Molten rock.

Mesozoic. Geologic time interval from about 245 to 66 million years ago.

metamorphic. A type of rock formed from heating up and squashing other existing rocks.

oil. Usually refers to dark liquid formed by old marine organisms like algae that were buried and transformed into a "fossil fuel" millions of years ago. We make gasoline, heating oil, plastic, and many other things from oil.

organism. Something living, or that was alive, like a plant or animal.

plutonic. Rock that crystallizes at depth beneath the Earth's surface.

tectonic plates. Huge "rafts of rock" at the solid outer layer of the Earth that fit together like a broken eggshell or jigsaw puzzle.

trilobite. Extinct animal that lived on the bottom of ancient seas (Ohio's state fossil).

sediment. Small, broken-up pieces of rocks or organisms.

sedimentary rock. A major rock type formed by sediment piling up, compressing, and becoming cemented together.

Silurian. Geologic time period from about 438 to 408 million years ago.

tropical. Warm—like down near the equator.

volcano. Mountain or landform created when lava erupts onto the surface.

xenolith. Piece of existing rock that falls into and crystallizes in a chamber of magma—like a raisin in raisin bread.

WHERE TO SEE OHIO'S GEOLOGY

Listed below are places where you can hike through scenic areas, collect fossils, or visit archaeological or historical sites that have a geological focus. The facilities of the Ohio Geological Survey (Delaware County, Horace R. Collins Laboratory, 1-740-548-7348; Erie County, Lake Erie Geology Group, 1-419-626-4296; Franklin County, main office, 1-614-265-6576) have displays and information on geology. For additional information on the sites listed below, please contact the appropriate agency, not the Ohio Geological Survey. Material for this section is adapted from *Where to See Ohio's Geology,* GeoFacts no. 21, published by the Ohio Department of Natural Resources, Division of Geological Survey. The information is subject to change, and it is always a good idea to call ahead to your destination.

KEY

A	archaeology site
CP	city or county park
F	fossil collecting by permission only
H	historical site
MP	metropark
PR	permit required
PV	private
RR#	hike number from Ramey, *Fifty Hikes in Ohio* (see references)
S	scenic geology
$	access fee
< >	Web site address

ADAMS COUNTY

Davis Memorial State Nature Preserve (S)

Johnson Ridge (formerly Unity Woods)
    State Nature Preserve (S)

Serpent Mound State Memorial (A, S)

Strait Creek Prairie Bluff State Nature
    Preserve (S, PR)

Robert A. Whipple State Nature Preserve (S)

Buzzardroost Rock (S, PV)

Sparrowood Nature Area (S, PV)

ASHLAND COUNTY

Mohican State Park and State Forest (S, RR10)

Clear Fork Gorge State Nature Preserve (S)

ATHENS COUNTY

Burr Oak State Park (S, RR22)

Strouds Run State Park (S, RR28)

Desonier State Nature Preserve (S)

Gifford State Forest (S)

Acadia Cliffs State Wildlife Area (S)

Waterloo State Wildlife Experiment Station (S)

BELMONT COUNTY

Barkcamp State Park (S)

Raven Rocks (S)

BROWN COUNTY

Indian Creek State Wildlife Area (S)

BUTLER COUNTY

Hueston Woods State Park (S, F)

Governor Bebb Park (S, CP)

Miami and Erie Canal Park (H, CP)

Rentschler Forest Preserve (S, CP)

Miami University Geology Museum (1-513-529-3220, <http://www.cas.muohio.edu/limpermuseum/>)

CHAMPAIGN COUNTY

Cedar Bog State Nature Preserve (S)

Siegenthaler-Kaestner Esker State Nature Preserve (S)

Ohio Caverns (S, $, 1-937-465-4017, <http://www.cavern.com/ohiocaverns/>)

CLARK COUNTY

Snyder Park (S, CP)

CLERMONT COUNTY

East Fork State Park (S, RR38)

Stonelick State Park (S, F)

Cincinnati Nature Center (S, PV, $ on Sat. & Sun.)

CLINTON COUNTY

Cowan Lake State Park (S, F)

COLUMBIANA COUNTY

Beaver Creek State Park (S, H, RR12)

Sheepskin Hollow (formerly Little Beaver Creek) State Nature Preserve (S)

COSHOCTON COUNTY

Woodbury State Wildlife Area (S)

CUYAHOGA COUNTY

Cleveland Metroparks System (1-216-351-6300, <http://www.clemetparks.com>): Bedford Reservation-Tinkers Creek Gorge (S, MP), Big Creek (S, MP), Bradley Woods (S, MP), Brecksville Reservation (S, MP, RR13), Euclid Creek (S, MP), North Chagrin Reservation (S, MP), Rocky River Reservation (S, MP), South Chagrin Reservation (S, MP), Shaker Lakes Regional Nature Center (S, MP)

Cuyahoga Valley National Park (S, H, RR14, 1-216-524-1497, <http://www.nps.gov/cuva/>)

Cleveland Museum of Natural History ($, 1-216-231-4600 or 1-800-317-9155, <http://www.cmnh.org>)

DELAWARE COUNTY

Alum Creek State Park (S)

Highbanks (S, H, A, MP, RR7)

Blue Limestone Park (S, CP)

O'Shaughnessy Reservoir and Dam (S, CP)

Olentangy Indian Caverns (S, $, 1-740-548-7917, <http://www.olentangyindiancaverns.com/>)

ERIE COUNTY

Kelleys Island (S, H, A, RR47)

Glacial Grooves State Memorial (S, H)

Milan State Wildlife Area (S)

The Blue Hole at Castalia (S)

FAIRFIELD COUNTY

The Fairfield County Visitor and Convention Bureau (1-740-654-5929 or 1-800-626-1296 <http://www.visitfairfieldcountyoh.org/naturepreserves.html>)

Christmas Rocks State Nature Preserve (S, PR)

Rhododendron Cove State Nature Preserve (S, PR)

Shallenberger State Nature Preserve (S)

Wahkeena Nature Preserve (Ohio Historical Society) (S, H, $)

Rock Mill Dam State Wildlife Area (S)

Lockville Locks (H, CP)

Rising Park and Mount Pleasant (S, H, CP)

Tarlton Cross Mound (S, A)

FRANKLIN COUNTY

Columbus and Franklin County Metropolitan
Park District (1-614-891-0700): Blendon Woods
(S, MP), Highbanks (S, H, A, MP, RR7)

Friendship Park (S, CP)

Glen Echo Park (S, CP)

Griggs Reservoir and Dam (S, CP)

Hayden Run Falls (S, CP)

Indian Village Camp (S, H, CP)

Whetstone Park (S, CP)

Ohio Historical Center ($, 1-614-297-2300,
<http://www.ohiohistory.org>)

Ohio State University Orton Museum
(1-614-292-6896, <http://www.geology
.ohio-state.edu/facilities/museums>)

GALLIA COUNTY

Tycoon Lake State Wildlife Area (S)

Bob Evans Farm (S, H)

GEAUGA COUNTY

Aquilla Lake State Wildlife Area (S, H)

Big Creek Park (S, CP)

Metals Park (S, H, CP)

Thompson Ledge Park (S, CP)

GREENE COUNTY

John Bryan State Park (S, RR37)

Little Miami State Park (S)

Clifton Gorge State Nature Preserve (S, H,
RR37)

Travertine Fen State Nature Preserve (S, PR)

Glen Helen (S, H, A, PV, owned by Antioch
College, RR41, 1-937-769-1902,
<http://www.antioch.edu/glenhelen.html>)

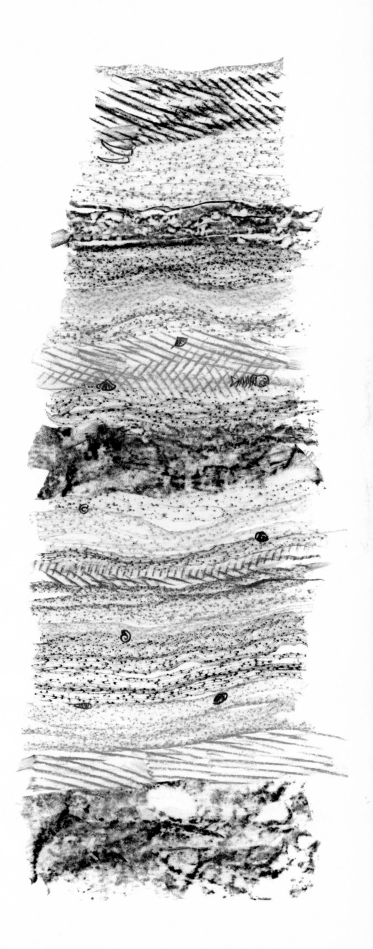

GUERNSEY COUNTY

Salt Fork State Park (S)

HAMILTON COUNTY

Hamilton County Park District (1-513-521-7275): Miami Whitewater Forest (S, H, $, MP), Sharon Woods (S, H, $, MP), Shawnee Lookout (S, A, $, MP, RR43), Winton Woods (S, $, MP)

Greenbelt State Nature Preserve (S, PR)

Newberry State Nature Preserve (S, PR)

Sharon Woods Gorge State Nature Preserve (S)

Cincinnati Museum of Natural History ($, 1-513-287-7000 or 1-800-733-2077, <http://www.cincymuseum.org>)

University of Cincinnati Geology Museum (1-513-556-3732)

HARRISON COUNTY

Harrison State Reclamation Area (S, H)

Tappan Lake Park (S, RR20)

History of Coal Museum (1-740-942-2623)

HIGHLAND COUNTY

Paint Creek State Park (S)

Rocky Fork State Park (S)

Fort Hill State Memorial (S, A, $, RR39)

Etawah Woods State Nature Preserve (S, PR, guided tours)

Miller State Nature Preserve (S, PR)

Fallsville State Wildlife Area (S, H)

Barrett's Mill (S, H)

Seven Caves (S, H, $, 1-937-365-1283)

HOCKING COUNTY

Hocking Hills State Park (S, RR8, Hocking Hills information: 1-740-385-9706 or 1-800-HOCKING, <http://www.hockinghills.com>): Ash Cave, Cantwell Cliffs, Cedar Falls, Conkle's Hollow State Nature Preserve (RR5), Old Man's Cave (H, A), Rock House

Tar Hollow State Park (S, RR29)

Clear Creek (formerly Allen F. Beck) State Nature Preserve (S)

Crane Hollow State Nature Preserve (S, PR)

Little Rocky Hollow State Nature Preserve (S, PR)

Rockbridge State Nature Preserve (S)

Sheick Hollow State Nature Preserve (S, PR)

Wayne National Forest (S, RR11)

HURON COUNTY

Augusta-Anne Olsen (formerly Vermilion River) State Nature Preserve (S, PR)

JACKSON COUNTY

Jackson Lake State Park (S)

Lake Katherine State Nature Preserve (S, RR24)

Buckeye Furnace State Memorial (S, H, $)

Leo Petroglyph State Memorial (S, A)

Cooper Hollow State Wildlife Area (S, RR23)

Liberty State Wildlife Area (S)

JEFFERSON COUNTY

Jefferson Lake State Park (S)

Brush Creek State Wildlife Area (S)

Fernwood State Forest (S)

KNOX COUNTY

Brinkhaven Access Wildlife Preserve (S)

LAKE COUNTY

Chapin Forest Reservation (S, MP)

Hogback Ridge Park (S, H, A, MP)

Indian Point Park (S, A, MP)

Headlands Dunes State Nature Preserve (S)

Holden Arboretum (S, PV)

LAWRENCE COUNTY

Dean State Forest (S)

Wayne National Forest (S, RR31)

LICKING COUNTY

Black Hand Gorge State Nature Preserve (S, H, A, RR3)

Flint Ridge State Memorial (S, H, A, $)

Octagon Earthworks and Moundbuilders Earthworks (A, $)

LOGAN COUNTY

Campbell Hill (S)

Zane Shawnee Caverns (S, $, 1-937-592-9592)

LORAIN COUNTY

Black River Reservation (S, MP)

Indian Hollow Reservation (S, H, MP)

Vermilion River Reservation (S, H, MP)

LUCAS COUNTY

Metroparks of the Toledo Area (1-419-535-3058 ext. 101, <http://www.metroparkstoledo.com>): Farnsworth Metropark (S, MP), Oak Openings Preserve (S, MP), Secor Metropark (F, MP), Maumee Bay State Park

MAHONING COUNTY

Mill Creek Park (S, H)

MEDINA COUNTY

Lodi City Park (F, CP)

Hinckley Reservation (S, CP, RR18)

MEIGS COUNTY

Forked Run State Park (S)

Shade River State Forest (S)

Belleville Locks and Dam (S, H, CP)

MIAMI COUNTY

Miami County Park District (1-937-667-1086): Charleston Falls Preserve (S, MP, RR36)

Ludlow Falls (S)

Overlook Falls (S)

Greenville Falls State Nature Preserve (S)

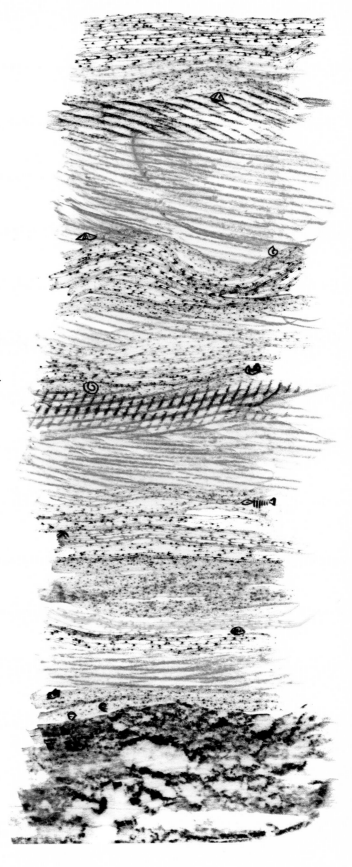

MONROE COUNTY

Rothenbuhler Woods State Nature Preserve (S, PR)

Sunfish Creek State Forest (S)

MONTGOMERY COUNTY

Dayton-Montgomery County Park District
(1-937-278-8231): Englewood Reserve (S),
Germantown Reserve (S, RR40), Huffman
Reserve (S, H)

Taylorsville Reserve (S)

Boonshoft Museum of Discovery
($, 1-937-275-7432)

MORGAN COUNTY

Burr Oak State Park (S, RR22)

Ohio Power Recreation Area (S, RR25)

Wayne National Forest (RR30 & 32)

MORROW COUNTY

Mt. Gilead State Park (S)

MUSKINGUM COUNTY

Blue Rock State Park and State Forest (S)

Baughman Park (S, H)

NOBLE COUNTY

Wolf Run State Park (S)

Senecaville Lake (S)

OTTAWA COUNTY

Marblehead Lighthouse State Park (S, H)

South Bass Island State Park (S)

Crystal Cave-Heineman Winery (S, $,
1-419-285-2811)

Perry's Cave (S, $, 1-419-285-2405,
<http://www.perryscave.com>)

PERRY COUNTY

Perry State Reclamation Area (S, H)

Wayne National Forest (S, RR11 & 32)

PIKE COUNTY

Lake White State Park (S)

Pike Lake State Park (S)

Strait Creek Prairie Bluff State Nature Preserve
(S, PR)

Pike State Forest (S)

Cave Lake Park (S)

PORTAGE COUNTY

Nelson-Kennedy Ledges State Park (S)

PREBLE COUNTY

Hueston Woods State Park (S, F)

Rush Run State Wildlife Area (S)

Fort St. Clair State Memorial (S)

Imes Park (S, CP)

RICHLAND COUNTY

Hemlock Falls (S, CP)

ROSS COUNTY

Great Seal State Park (S, H)

Scioto Trail State Park and State Forest (S, H,
RR26)

Tar Hollow State Park and State Forest (S, RR29)

Hopewell Culture National Historical Park (S, A,
H, $)

Seip Mound (S, A, H, $)

Copperas Mountain (S)

SANDUSKY COUNTY

Miller Blue Hole (S)

SCIOTO COUNTY

Shawnee State Park and State Forest (S, RR27)

Raven Rock State Nature Preserve (S, PR)

SENECA COUNTY

Seneca Caverns (S, $, 1-419-483-6711,
<http://www.senecacavernsohio.com>)

STARK COUNTY

McKinley Museum of Science and Technology ($, 1-330-455-7043, <http://www.mckinleymuseum.org>)

SUMMIT COUNTY

Summit County Metro Parks (1-330-867-5511): Deep Lock Quarry (S, H, MP), Furnace Run (S, F, MP), Gorge Metropark (S, H), Virginia Kendall Metropark (S)

Adell Durban Park and Arboretum (S, CP)

Cuyahoga Valley National Park (S, H, RR14, 1-216-524-1497, <http://www.nps.gov/cuva/>)

Hale Farm and Village (S, PV)

TUSCARAWAS COUNTY

Devil's Den Park (S, H, CP)

Zoar Lake (S, H)

VINTON COUNTY

Lake Alma State Park (S)

Lake Hope State Park and Zaleski State Forest (S, H, RR33)

Tar Hollow State Park and State Forest (S, RR29)

WARREN COUNTY

Caesar Creek State Park (F, H)

Little Miami State Park (S)

Caesar Creek Gorge State Nature Preserve (S)

Halls Creek Woods State Nature Preserve (S)

Fort Ancient State Memorial (A, $)

WASHINGTON COUNTY

Acadia Cliffs State Wildlife Area (S)

Boord State Nature Preserve (S)

Ladd Natural Bridge State Nature Preserve (S, PR)

Wayne National Forest (S, RR30)

WAYNE COUNTY

Spangler Park (S, CP)

Ken Miller's Oil and Gas Museum (PV, call ahead: 330-264-9146)

WOOD COUNTY

Ostego Park (S, CP)

Steidtman Wildlife Sanctuary (S, PV)

WYANDOT COUNTY

Indian Trail Caverns (S, PV, $, 1-419-387-7773, <http://www.indian-trail-caverns.com/>)

These are just some of the many places to
see Ohio's geology, but there are rocks and
fossils under your feet in your own backyard—
you can start by looking there!

REFERENCES

Much of the information for this book is from the publications of the Ohio Department of Natural Resources (DNR), Division of Geological Survey. Anyone wanting to learn more about Ohio's geology should check out the GeoFacts series and other publications of the DNR, many of which are available on the DNR Web site at http://www.dnr.state.oh.us/geosurvey/geo-fact/.

Specific references used in this book include the following:

Coogan, Alan H. "Ohio's Surface Rocks and Sediments." Paper, modified from chapter 3 of *Fossils of Ohio,* edited by Rodney M. Feldmann and Merrianne Hackathorn. Ohio Geological Survey Bulletin 70. Columbus: Ohio DNR, Division of Geological Survey, 1996.

Crowell, Douglas L. *Coal.* Modified from Educational Leaflet no. 8. Columbus: Ohio DNR, Division of Geological Survey, 2000.

Hansen, Michael C. *Earthquakes in Ohio.* Educational Leaflet no. 9. Columbus: Ohio DNR, Division of Geological Survey, 2005.

———, comp. *The Geology of Ohio—The Precambrian.* GeoFacts no. 13. Columbus: Ohio DNR, Division of Geological Survey, 1996.

Ohio Department of Natural Resources, Division of Geological Survey. *A Brief Summary of the Geologic History of Ohio.* GeoFacts no. 23. Columbus: Ohio DNR, Division of Geological Survey, 2001.

———. *Clay and Shale in Ohio.* Educational Leaflet no. 12. Columbus: Ohio DNR, Division of Geological Survey, 2005.

———. Map of Glacial Deposits of Ohio. Columbus: Ohio DNR, Division of Geological Survey.

———. Map of Ohio Karst Areas. Columbus: Ohio DNR, Division of Geological Survey.

Ohio Historical Society. *Ohio's Geologic Timeline.* Columbus: Ohio Historical Society, 2005.

Plummer, Charles C., David McGeary, and Diane H. Carlson. *Physical Geology* (New York: McGraw-Hill, 2005).

Ramey, Ralph. *Fifty Hikes in Ohio: Walks, Hikes, and Backpacking Trips throughout the Buckeye State.* Woodstock, VT: Backcountry Publications, 1990.

Shrake, Douglas L., comp. *Fossil Collecting in Ohio.* GeoFacts no. 17. Columbus: Ohio DNR, Division of Geological Survey, 2000.

United States Geologic Survey. "Ohio." *America's Volcanic Past.* http://vulcan.wr .usgs.gov/LivingWith/VolcanicPast/Places/volcanic_past_ohio.html.

OHIO GEOLOGICAL
EXPLORATION FIELD NOTES

Explorer: _____

Date: _____

Time: _____

Location: _____

(Draw map below)

Observations and discoveries made:

North

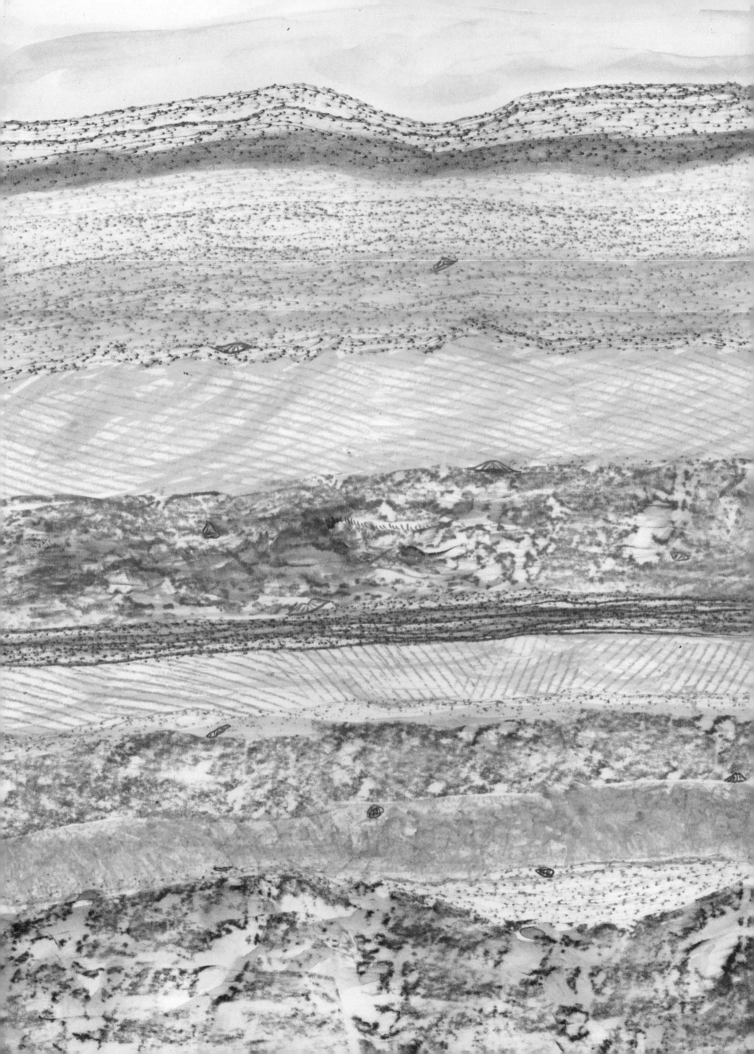